FIGHTING FOR THEIR COUNTRY:
MINORITIES AT WAR

Minority Soldiers Fighting in World War II

MATT LANG

Cavendish Square
New York

Published in 2018 by Cavendish Square Publishing, LLC
243 5th Avenue, Suite 136, New York, NY 10016

First Edition

CPSIA Compliance Information: Batch #CS17CSQ

All websites were available and accurate when this book was sent to press.

Library of Congress Cataloging-in-Publication Data

Names: Lang, Matt.
Title: Minority soldiers fighting in World War II / Matt Lang.
Description: New York : Cavendish Square, 2018. | Series: Fighting for their country: minorities at war | Includes index.
Identifiers: ISBN 9781502626646 (library bound) | ISBN 9781502626585 (ebook)
Subjects: LCSH: World War, 1939-1945--Participation, African American--Juvenile literature. | World War, 1939-1945--African Americans--Juvenile literature. | United States. Army Air Forces. Fighter Squadron, 99th--History--Juvenile literature.
Classification: LCC D810.N4 L36 2018 | DDC 940.54'03--dc23

Editorial Director: David McNamara
Editor: Caitlyn Miller
Copy Editor: Alex Tessman
Associate Art Director: Amy Greenan
Designer: Stephanie Flecha
Production Coordinator: Karol Szymczuk
Photo Research: J8 Media

The photographs in this book are used by permission and through the courtesy of:
Cover Bettmann/Getty Images; p. 4 Epics/Hulton Archive/Getty Images; New York Times Company/Archive Photos/Getty Images; p. 13 Hulton-Deutsch Collection/Corbis/Getty Images; pp. 16, 23, 57, 73 Bettmann/Getty Images; pp. 25, 37, 41, 78 Corbis/Getty Images; p. 28 Galerie Bilderwelt/Hulton Archive/Getty Images; p. 30 The Print Collector/Getty Images; pp. 44, 48 Universal History Archive/UIG/Getty Images; p. 47 Central Press/Hulton Archive/Getty Images; p. 50 USAAF/File: Boeing Stearman at Tuskegee Airfield c1942.jpg/Wikimedia Commons; p. 52 File: Booker T. Washington by Francis Benjamin Johnston, c. 1895.jpg/Wikimedia Commons; p. 55 Author unknown/File: "Keep us flying! Buy War Bonds." - NARA - 514823.jpg/Wikimedia Commons; p. 63 Myron Davis/The LIFE Picture Collection/Getty Images; p. 66 Leonard McCombe/The LIFE Images Collection/Getty Images; p. 69 Major General Clayton B. Vogel, United States Marine Corps/File: Navaho-enlistment-letter-page01 &02.jpg /Wikimedia Commons; p. 75 George Rinhart/Corbis/Getty Images; p. 82 Douglas Graham/Roll Call/Getty Images; p. 85 Underwood Archives/Getty Images; p. 86 Robert Abbott Sengstacke/Getty Images; p. 89 Gage Skidmore/File: Dolores Huerta (25854563002).jpg/Wikimedia Commons; p. 91 Joseph Sohm/Corbis/Getty Images; p. 93 The U.S. National Archives/File: We Can Do It! (3678696585).jpg/Wikimedia Commons.

Printed in the United States of America

CONTENTS

Total War

In the early morning of December 7, 1941, Japanese bombers attacked the United States Naval Fleet stationed in Pearl Harbor, Hawaii. More than three hundred Japanese fighter planes sank four United States battle ships and damaged four others. The Japanese also damaged or sank cruisers, destroyers, and anti-aircraft ships, and destroyed 188 aircraft. Ultimately, the attack killed 2,403 Americans and injured 1,178 others. These figures contrast sharply with the Japanese casualties: they lost only twenty-nine airplanes and sixty-four people. The next day, December 8, the United States declared war on Japan and thus entered World War II.

Until the attack on Pearl Harbor, most people in the United States did not support joining the war, which began in 1939 when Nazi Germany invaded Poland. After the invasion, France and the United Kingdom declared war on Germany. From 1939 to 1941, Germany took control of much of Europe

***Opposite*: The attack on Pearl Harbor**

and formed an alliance with Italy and Japan. This alliance was known as the **Axis**, and together they took control of not only most of Europe, but also pushed into the former Soviet Union and North Africa. Japanese forces, which had invaded China in 1937, moved farther into mainland Asia and farther into the Pacific.

After Pearl Harbor, public opinion shifted, and most of America supported the war effort. The United States joined with the United Kingdom, the Soviet Union, the Free French, and China to form the **Allies**. Other Allies included the Netherlands, Australia, Belgium, Greece, Mexico, and Poland. In all, more than 100 million people from more than thirty countries took part in the war. By the time the war ended in 1945, between 60 to 80 million people were killed, two-thirds of them civilians. The total number of dead equaled 3 percent of the world's population in 1940. No war before or since has been so deadly.

The major combatants, like the United States, the United Kingdom, and Germany, were in a state of total war. Almost all the resources of each nation were put into the war effort—even industries like agriculture and entertainment became part of the conflict. Though there were no battles fought on land in the United States, every citizen was asked contribute. Hollywood studios encouraged movie stars to **enlist**, professional athletes left their teams to fly planes, families were encouraged to plant victory gardens and buy war bonds, and every manufacturing facility was used to produce equipment for the war. There were no new cars, appliances, furniture, or houses built during the war. Food and gasoline were **rationed**, and wages and prices were strictly controlled. Taxes were raised to an all-time high, and people saved record percentages of their income. Women entered the workforce in numbers never seen before, as did teenagers—both groups were sorely needed to replace the men who went off to fight. Farmers were mostly exempt from the draft, though many left their farms to volunteer for the war or to work in factories in cities.

In 1940, the total population of the United States was 131,669,275. Around 116,261,189 people were white, or almost 89 percent of the population. African Americans made up just under 10 percent of the total population, at 12,865,518 people, Hispanics comprised 1.5 percent of the of those living in America, with 2,021,820 people. Native Americans made up 0.3 percent of the population (333,969 people), and 0.2 percent of the population identified as Asian or Pacific Islanders (254,918 people).

Despite accounting for such a small percentage of the population, each of these groups made a significant contribution to the war effort. Minority soldiers and civilians often fought for rights that they themselves did not enjoy. For example, the Tuskegee Airmen were the nation's first African American fighter pilots, but before they could fight against the Axis, they had to fight against the discrimination that kept them out of the military. Overall, 125,000 African Americans enlisted in the military, which was still segregated at the time.

Between 250,000 and 500,000 Hispanics served in World War II. Their service was done in spite of the fact that Mexican Americans and other Hispanics were discriminated against and distrusted at home. In 1943, when so many Hispanics were fighting and dying overseas, Mexican American youths in Los Angeles were attacked by white Americans, including servicemen. The **Zoot Suit** Riots, as the attacks were known, sparked a wave of similar attacks in cities across the United States.

In 1939, the median income for Native American males was $500, compared to $2,300 for the average male nationwide. There was little opportunity for employment and education on **reservations**. Regardless of their marginal status—or perhaps because of it—Native Americans joined the military in large numbers relative to their population. Approximately 25,000 men enlisted, one-third of the population of able-bodied men age 18–50. On top of that, several hundred Native American women worked as nurses.

The most significant contribution of Native Americans to the war effort was the work of the Navajo code talkers. The code talkers translated English words into the Navajo language, a complex language unknown in most of the world. Once translated into Navajo, messages could be sent without the fear that they might be decoded by the enemy.

With the United States at war with Japan, people of Japanese ancestry were viewed with great suspicion by the public, and even by the United States government. Eventually, Japanese Americans, even those who had been in the country for generations, were forced to live in **internment camps** for the duration of the war. However, even though their Constitutional rights were violated, many Japanese Americans willingly and bravely served. The 442nd Regimental Combat Team was made up of soldiers of Japanese descent. The 442nd fought in Italy and France and were commended for their skill and bravery.

This book will look at what life was like at home before the war for these different minority groups, look closer at the war itself, and explain the tireless contributions of the Tuskegee Airmen and the Navajo code talkers, which helped the Allies win the war. Finally, we will look at what happened when these soldiers came back home to a country that did not always celebrate the difference they had made.

PARAMOUNT THEATRE
COLORED ENTRANCE
Enjoy Good Shows in Comfort

ONE

Life at Home

Even though they fought for their country overseas, minority soldiers did not enjoy the same rights and freedoms as white soldiers. Racism was often codified in the laws of the time, and minorities faced overwhelming obstacles to equality.

JIM CROW

By the late 1830s, Jim Crow was being used as a racial slur against black people. Eventually, it became the informal name for a system of laws and customs that operated mostly, but not exclusively, in the South. After the Civil War (1861–1865), there was a period known as Reconstruction, during which newly freed blacks were given new rights by the Thirteenth, Fourteenth, and Fifteenth Amendments to the Constitution. When Reconstruction ended in 1877, a series of laws—"Black Codes"—were passed to strip African Americans of these

***Opposite*: During World War II, the southern states were still segregated.**

rights. These laws were passed primarily in the Southern states, though they were in place in other parts of the country as well. The name Jim Crow was taken from a minstrel song:

> *Come listen all you galls and boys,*
> *I'm going to sing a little song,*
> *My name is Jim Crow.*
> *Weel about and turn about and do jis so,*
> *Eb'ry time I weel about I jump Jim Crow. (sic)"*

The song was written by Thomas Dartmouth "Daddy" Rice, a white musician who performed in makeup known as blackface. Such performances were known as minstrel shows, and they portrayed black people as lazy, stupid, and foolish.

Jim Crow laws were the basis for **segregation** in the South. These laws said that blacks and whites had to have separate schools, separate bathrooms, and separate drinking fountains, among other separate amenities. Jim Crow laws also made it difficult, if not impossible, for African Americans to vote, serve on juries, run for office, or otherwise participate in public life. Jim Crow laws were still firmly in place in before, during, and after World War II.

Even in the military, discrimination was a way of life. Black soldiers were denied the same training and opportunities as white soldiers, and opportunities for African Americans to become pilots were almost nonexistent. In 1939, the year World War II began in Europe, there were only twenty-five licensed pilots in the United States. After the United States entered the war, soldiers from all walks of life began enlisting or being drafted. Civil rights organizations, such as the

Many Navajo people died during this forced migration, which they called the Long Walk. By the time the Navajo were finally allowed to return to their land in 1868, most moved to the Navajo reservation.

Others moved nearby and bought plots of land on which to build small houses and raise sheep and goats; this area came to be known as the Checkerboard. Chester Nez, who was one of the last surviving code talkers, recalls his childhood growing up in the Checkerboard Area, a region of New Mexico near the Navajo Reservation: "We would go for three days or four days without eating. Everything always comes last to the Checkerboard." At the start of World War II, even as native people like Nez were volunteering for the military, many were not even allowed to vote. In New Mexico, for example, native people could not vote.

The Great Depression and the Dust Bowl Era of the 1930s hit the Navajo reservation hard, and government policies that were part of the New Deal did not help much. Nevertheless, when fighting broke out in Europe, even before the United States entered the war, the Navajo Tribal Council passed a unanimous resolution which ended with these words:

> *Now, therefore, we resolve that the Navajo Indians stand ready as they did in 1918, to aid and defend our Government and its institutions against all subversive and armed conflict and pledge our loyalty to the system which recognizes minority rights and a way of life that has placed us among the great people of our race.*

The Abraham Lincoln Brigade

The Spanish Civil war took place between 1936 and 1939. The war was fought between the Republicans, who were loyal to Spanish **Republic** (the left-leaning, elected government in power at the time), and the **fascist** Nationalists. In many ways, the war was a prelude to World War II, with the Nationalists receiving aid from Germany and Italy, and the Republicans getting help from the Soviet Union and Mexico.

The Republicans also got help from volunteers from the United States. Though the United States did not officially intervene in the war, and, in fact, the State Department tried to prevent citizens from traveling to Spain, approximately 2,800 people from the United States traveled to Spain to join the fight. Among the 2,800 were ninety African American fighters, including two women.

The volunteers from America were grouped with volunteers from England, Canada, Ireland, and Latin America into the Fifteenth Brigade. Those from the United States, thinking of their own country's struggles for freedom, named their battalions Lincoln and Washington. The Lincoln Brigade, which included the African American volunteers, was integrated at a time when the United States Army was still segregated. In Spain, African American soldiers were given leadership opportunities that they would not have been given otherwise, and most African American fighters signed up because they saw the war as a chance to fight against some of the same kind of racial prejudice and injustice that they experienced in America.

Most members of the Lincoln Brigade were leftist, and some were **Communists**. When members of the Brigade returned home, they were regarded with suspicion and considered security risks during World War II, though some went on to serve in the US military and fight in the war. One, Edgar A. Carter Jr., was later awarded with a Medal of Honor.

THE HISPANIC EXPERIENCE

In 1940, when President Roosevelt ordered the first peacetime draft in the nation's history, the first person selected was Pedro Aguilar Despart, a Mexican American from East Los Angeles. Approximately 500,000 Latinos would fight in World War II, some of them recent immigrants, some whose families had been in the country for generations. Much like black soldiers, however, Latino soldiers were fighting for a country that didn't treat them as equals.

Eugene Calderon was one example. Born in Puerto Rico but living in New York in the 1920s, Calderon enlisted in the military to learn how to fly. The army sent him to Tuskegee, where he initially roomed with the white officers, who complained that he wasn't white. He was moved in with the black officers, who were upset because he wasn't black. Eventually, he was moved to another **barrack**, this one with another Latino. They were the only two men in the barrack.

Growing up in New York, surrounded by other Puerto Ricans, blacks, Italians, Jewish people, Irish people, and many others, Calderon rarely thought about the realities of discrimination. Yet in the military he not only experienced discrimination in housing, but also in training and opportunity. In order to limit the number of nonwhite pilots, the military would transfer pilots who were close to completing their certification. Once they were transferred, they had to begin the process all over again. When Calderon got close to meeting his requirements, he was transferred from Tuskegee to a base in South Dakota.

The Bracero Program

The United States went to war in 1941. By 1942, with so many men at war, there was a labor shortage, both in factories and on farms. In many cases, women joined the workforce like never before, but even with their labor, there will still many jobs to fill. Without enough farm workers, people worried that crops, which were needed to feed soldiers all around the world, would rot in the fields.

In August of 1942, the United States and Mexican governments signed an agreement for one million temporary workers to move from Mexico to the United States. The move would be paid for by the United States, and, as part of the agreement, the Mexicans workers, known as **braceros**, would to be given basic protections against mistreatment. By the end of the war, over 300,000 Mexican men had worked in the Bracero Program.

Under the provisions of the program, braceros were to be given housing, safe working conditions, occupational insurance in case they were injured on the job, a wage of not less than 30 cents an hour, and travel to and from Mexico. These conditions were not strictly enforced, however, and many *braceros* worked long hours for little pay in hazardous conditions.

Though the program was necessary for the war effort, many Americans resented the *braceros*, who they accused of taking advantage of government assistance and taking away American jobs. The poor working conditions, the hostility of many Americans, and the workers' unfamiliarity with American culture kept the *braceros* isolated from the majority.

At the same time, workers were flocking to large cities like Los Angeles, drawn by manufacturing jobs in support of the war effort. Many of these workers were young Latinos, excited to be getting a steady paycheck for the first time in their lives. With more money, and some free time, young Mexican American workers went out on the town, dressed in nice new suits.

The Zoot Suit Riots

One of the favorite styles of the time was the zoot suit. With baggy, high-waisted pants and long jackets with wide shoulders, the zoot suit was popular in the late thirties and early forties. But as war time rations took hold and Americans were encouraged to cut back on everything from driving to eating meat, the zoot suit came to be seen as a waste of fabric that a nation at war could not afford to produce.

Even though it was officially banned, zoot suits continued to be produced by bootleg tailors, and they continued to be worn by young men eager to form their own identity in new surroundings, in opposition to the identity of their parents and other authority figures. Members of the Mexican working-class subculture eager to forge counter-culture identities were known as ***pachucos***. Along with the zoot suits, they also had their own slang and distinct hair-dos. All of these characteristics were meant to defiantly set them apart from the mainstream.

As the war escalated, so too did fear of foreigners and worries about enemy infiltration. In California, there were rumors that Nazis were actively recruiting Mexicans. In Los Angeles, the streets were full of *pachucos* in zoot suits and young sailors and soldiers either home on leave or waiting to be

Mexican youths jokingly "surrender" during the Zoot Suit Riots of 1943.

deployed. This volatile combination erupted on June 3, 1943, when a sailor accused a *pachuco* of lunging at him. A fight broke out, which escalated into days and nights of unrest between men in uniform and men in zoot suits. Over the course of the next ten days, servicemen would attack *pachucos* in the street, strip them of their clothes, and light their clothes on fire. From Los Angeles, the violence spread to Pasadena, Long Beach, San Diego, Phoenix, and several other cities.

Though investigations would eventually conclude that sailors started the riots, no sailors were arrested. Yet over five hundred Latinos were charged with assault, vagrancy, and other crimes. As activist Jose Angel Gutierrez later pointed out:

> *This was happening as the United States was fighting the Nazis. America was supposed to stand for tolerance, for equality. Yet servicemen were bashing ... other Americans because they weren't the standard-issue white Americans—at a time when Mexican Americans were making a mighty contribution to the war effort. These beatings and humiliation colored the worldview of generations of Latinos to come.*

JAPANESE INTERNMENT

After the attack on Pearl Harbor, Japanese Americans came under intense suspicion. Even people whose families had been in the country for generations were suspected of being spies or otherwise working for the Japanese. The suspicion even spread to Congress. Said one Congressman, "I'm for catching every Japanese in America ... now and putting them in concentration camps ... damn them! Let's get rid of them!"

Japanese American children parade in front of a Liberty Bell float, even as they were being held in an internment camp.

Though President Roosevelt was not as verbally hysterical about the perceived threat, he still signed Executive Order 9066 in February 1942. This order gave the army the power to arrest every Japanese American on the West Coast: 110,000 people, including children. Japanese immigrants and Japanese Americans could be arrested without a warrant and held without a hearing. They were taken from their homes and moved into camps where they lived in prison-like conditions. Most of the people in

Daniel Inouye lived in an internment camp as a child. He went on to serve in World War II and was later elected to the Senate.

the internment camps were children born in the United States to Japanese parents. By virtue of being born in the United States, they were American citizens. They remainder of the detainees were born in Japan, and under the executive order were barred from becoming citizens. The Supreme Court ruled that the internment was unconstitutional but they allowed it because it was, they said, a legal necessity.

After Pearl Harbor, many Americans, including government officials, feared that war would come to American shores. Many people were blaming anyone who was Japanese or Japanese American. Yuri Kochiyama, who survived life in the internment camps, remembers the anti-Japanese hysteria at the time. It seemed to her that the entire country was against her. "If there was anyone for the Japanese, you didn't hear about it. I'm sure they were afraid to speak out, because they would be considered … unpatriotic."

Families that went into the camps didn't think they would have to stay long, but as time went by, their frustration grew. Even worse, many families were split apart, with some being sent to one camp, and some to another. Still, they never lost their sense of identity or pride in their heritage.

TWO

The War Itself

By the time World War II came to the United States with the bombing of Pearl Harbor in 1941, it had been raging for years in Europe and Asia. The war in Europe began in Europe on September 1, 1939, when Germany invaded Poland. France and the United Kingdom then declared war on Germany. In Asia, Japan, looking to expand its Empire across the Pacific, invaded China in 1937.

EUROPE

The seeds of the conflict in Europe were sown in the aftermath of World War I, which ended in 1919 with the **Treaty** of Versailles. Under the terms of the treaty, Germany was forced to give up some of its territory and pay war reparations. Though the German government, known as the Weimar Republic, was able to negotiate to get many of the reparations lowered, their impact was made worse by the Great Depression. Added to

Opposite: The German military used panzer tanks to attack quickly.

Adolph Hitler rose to power with a promise to restore Germany to glory.

that was hyperinflation of the German currency, and a young, unstable political system.

The Weimar Republic was the unofficial name given to the German state that was established in 1919 following

World War I and a revolution in Germany that replaced the imperial government with a democratic republic. The republic was never able to fully unite Germany and was faced with political extremism on both sides. Many people blamed it for Germany's loss in World War I and the terms of the Versailles treaty, even though it was not in power at the time.

The instability of the Weimar Republic, the suffering brought on by the Great Depression, and the lingering humiliation of the Treaty of Versailles all came together to create a national mood that was ripe for an **authoritarian** ruler.

Adolph Hitler came to power promising to restore Germany's glory by uniting not only the people of Germany, but all the Germanic peoples of Europe into a larger German nation. Hitler promised to acquire *lebenstraum,* or "living space," new territory that could be populated by German settlers. This new territory would be found mostly to the east of Germany, in nations such as Poland.

Hitler also blamed Jewish people for Germany's problems, claiming they weakened German institutions and profited from Germany suffering, and he began to crack down on others he labelled political opponents as well. He organized a secret paramilitary group known as the Brownshirts who harassed and terrorized opposition figures. Soon after he became chancellor of Germany in 1933, he outlawed meetings of the German Communist Party. Not long after that, the Reichstag (the parliament building) caught fire under mysterious circumstances. Hitler used the burning of the Reichstag as an excuse to unleash the Brownshirts and the Storm Troopers, another paramilitary group, to make thousands of arrests of political opponents.

Hitler then invaded Eastern Europe, assuring his opponents that each step would be his last. After invading the Rhineland in 1936 and Austria in 1938, he then set his sights on Czechoslovakia. After the invasion of Czechoslovakia, Hitler invited British Prime Minister Neville Chamberlin, French Prime Minister Edouard Daladier, and Italian Premier Benito Mussolini to a meeting in Europe. On September 30 of that year, those leaders signed the Munich **Pact**. The pact said that the Czechs were to move out of the region known as the Sudentenland beginning in October of 1938. By March of 1939, German had control of Prague and the whole of Czechoslovakia. As he had many times before, Hitler claimed that Germany would make no other claims on any other territory.

However, no sooner had Germany taken control of Czechoslovakia than Hitler began laying the groundwork for the invasion of Poland. He claimed that Germans—the "master race," according to Hitler—were being mistreated by the "inferior" Polish people. Particularly upsetting to Hitler was the existence of the Polish Corridor. The corridor was given to Poland when the European map was redrawn after the First World War. The purpose of the corridor was to give Poland access to the sea. The corridor divided the rest of Germany from the province of East Prussia. The area was chosen because it has a majority Polish population. The coastal city of Danzig, made up of mostly Germans, was considered a semi-**autonomous** region, controlled by neither Poland or Germany.

Both France and Britain warned Germany that they would side with Poland if Germany invaded. However, Hitler was

Harry Truman became president of the United States after the death of President Franklin Delano Roosevelt.

The bombings of Hiroshima and Nagasaki resulted in the almost complete destruction of both cities.

On August 6, 1945, an American B-29 bomber, nicknamed the *Enola Gay* after the pilot's mother, dropped a nuclear bomb on the industrial city of Hiroshima. The blast destroyed 90 percent of the city and killed eighty thousand people instantly. Still, the Japanese did not surrender. On August 9, another B-29 dropped a second bomb on the city of Nagasaki, killing forty thousand more people. Hundreds of thousands more would later die of radiation sickness from the bombings. On August 15, the Japanese surrendered to the United States.

The two bombs were the first nuclear weapons used in war. No others have been used since.

28

THREE

The Tuskegee Airmen

Tuskegee, Alabama, in Macon county, developed as an important cotton trading center in the nineteenth century, but by the 1880s, the economy was declining and the town was losing population. Though white leaders did everything they could to keep African Americans out of power, they also realized that they could not reverse the town's decline without the help of black labor. The most ardent racists opposed giving black people any kind services, but others were willing to build a separate school for African Americans if it meant it would keep enough black workers from moving away.

THE TUSKEGEE INSTITUTE

The Tuskegee Institute opened in 1881 and hired Booker T. Washington as the principal. Washington was the son of a white man and an enslaved woman. Washington never met his father, but his mother and others around him raised him to believe in

Opposite: Tuskegee Airfield

Booker T. Washington, a firm believer in the power of education, was the first principal of the Tuskegee Institute.

the power of hard work and education. Under Washington's leadership, the Tuskegee Institute focused on teaching industrial arts and preparing graduates to be laborers and farmers, which Washington believed were the more important skills for black students to learn.

The Tuskegee Institute rose to national prominence and was successful even though it was controversial. Critics claimed the institute and Washington compromised too much with segregationists in the South, while proponents said it was a pragmatic approach that brought real progress to the black community. In 1935, Dr. Frederick Douglass Patterson was president of Tuskegee Institute, and he supported teaching aviation for these same pragmatic reasons. He wanted students to learn to be pilots, and also mechanics, air traffic controllers, and flight instructors. Under his leadership, Tuskegee became the first historically black college to offer aviation as part of the curriculum. When the war effort expanded after Pearl Harbor and the decision was made to train black pilots, the Tuskegee Institute was the natural choice for the location of the training.

JOINING THE FIGHT

Two years after the first cadet class began training at Tuskegee, the 99th Fighter **Squadron** received their orders to deploy. There was excitement, there was pride, and there was also plenty of fear. No one in the squadron had any combat experience, so no one knew what to expect.

The squadron was deployed to North Africa. From New York, they set sail for Casablanca, Morocco, on the U.S.S. *Mariposa.* Colonel Benjamin O. Davis was the ranking commander on the ship, which also carried thousands of white servicemen. It was probably the first time in US history that a black officer was in charge of white troops.

Colonel Davis was a graduate of the United States Military Academy at West Point. During his four years at West Point, Davis never had a roommate, always ate by himself in the mess hall, and was given the silent treatment by the rest of the cadets. In spite of this, he succeeded, never losing faith in himself: "I was better than anybody else in the things I was interested in doing. No doubt in my mind whatsoever," he later said. The other cadets were giving him the silent treatment, he knew, "because they did not want blacks at West Point." He refused to let the treatment get to him, though: "I was stubborn enough to put up with their treatment to reach the goal I had come to attain … I maintained my self-respect."

After he graduated, Davis went to Fort Benning in Georgia, then to Tuskegee. In both places, he lived with the reality of segregation. Though he was promoted quickly, he was unhappy at Tuskegee. His work was unsatisfying, and he felt unproductive. He left when he had the chance to transfer, but he came back after he was asked to take command of the 99th squadron.

Members of the 99th flew their first combat mission two months after they arrived in North Africa. Flying alongside white pilots from the 33rd squadron, they dive-bombed German targets on the Italian island of Pantelleria. The Allies had pushed the German out of North Africa and were working towards an invasion of Italy. The bombing campaign was the first step toward that invasion.

Before they could invade the Italian mainland, the Allies invaded the island of Sicily in July 1943. The 99th was once

The Tuskegee Airmen were so popular that their images were used to sell war bonds.

again instrumental in that effort, fighting with the 33rd. By August 1943, the Allies controlled Sicily and the 99th was left on the island to patrol the airspace while the white pilots of the 33rd were sent to fight over the mainland. The 99th flew their missions, but there were no enemies to engage, and therefore no enemy aircraft to shoot down. Critics who were skeptical of the "experiment" of training black pilots used the lack of action as "proof" that African Americans made poor pilots.

One such skeptic was Colonel William Momyer, the commander of the 33rd. It was his decision to send the 33rd to fight over Italy and keep the 99th behind in Sicily. He then criticized the 99th for a lack of skill and "aggression." His report, which was leaked to the press before it reached the War Department Advisory Committee on Negro Troop Policies, also known as the McCloy Committee, almost put an end to the Tuskegee Airmen.

In it, he wrote: "It is my opinion that they are not of the fighting caliber of any squadron in the group. They have failed to display the aggressiveness and desire for combat that are necessary to a first class fighting organization."

Colonel Davis was given a chance to answer the charges. He defended the airmen, saying that any mistakes came not from a lack of skill or natural ability, but from a lack of experience. The more combat they saw, the better they flew. Davis was also upset that Momyer didn't tell him about the concerns he had with the airmen. Instead, he submitted a report before there was any chance for the airmen to respond to his complaints. Furthermore, they couldn't be "aggressive" if they weren't given missions in which to fight. They did what they were asked to do, nothing more, nothing less. As Davis testified, "I carried out my mission—if given a mission to bomb a target, I went ahead and bombed it."

After Davis's testimony, the War Department revisited Momyer's report and concluded it was not a fair or conclusive evaluation of the ability or performance of the 99th. A new,

A group of Tuskegee Airmen, dressed for combat

impartial report concluded that there was no difference between the 99th and any other squadron, and, in fact, the 99th had not been given the same opportunities as other fighters.

That changed when the Allies launched Operation Shingle, an invasion of the Mediterranean coast of Italy. Given the chance to prove themselves as equals in combat, the 99th shot down twelve German airplanes in two days. Their

"If It Had Not Been for Us …"

The battle for Iwo Jima was one of the most important and most intense battles in the Pacific. African American soldiers played an important role in the assault. Arthur Peterson was one of those soldiers. Here he describes the heat of battle:

> *We could see bullets flying through the air. The smell of gunpowder was everywhere. I didn't think we were going to make it. It seemed like the deafening sound of big guns and bombs exploding would never end. When I did go ashore in the later waves, the ground was littered with so many more casualties than I thought I would see.*
>
> *If it had not been for us [African-American soldiers], our situation would have been worse. We were the main line of supply for the artillery units for the lead assault division and we did our job by bringing the ammunition and supplies they needed so that they could keep fighting … [We] were a vital link between the troops ashore and the logistical support they needed to survive ashore, but recorded history has given them little credit for their service.*
>
> *After the battle my unit, along with other Army units stationed on ships offshore, came aboard the island after the Marines turned control of it over to the Army, and served as the occupation force until Iwo Jima was returned to the Japanese government.*

B-25 bombers, flying in formation

he transferred command of the 477th and Godman Field from Selway to Colonel Davis, making him the first black commanding officer of a stateside base.

The one hundred and one were free, but the other three—Roger Terry, Marsden Thomson, and Shirley Clinton—faced a court martial. Their cases drew the attention of the NAACP, black newspapers, and the general public. Clinton and Thomson

Benjamin O. Davis Jr., one of the original Tuskegee Airmen, and the first African American officer in the United States Air Force

were found not guilty of all charges, but Terry was tried separately. The prosecutor asked for the death penalty for Terry on all charges.

The jury found Terry guilty of pushing an officer on his way into Officers' Club No. 2, but not guilty of the more serious charge of disobeying a direct order. He was fined $150 and held on the base for three months. After that, he was free to go. It was a big victory for Terry and black servicemen. The light sentence was an acknowledgement that Terry and the others had a right to be in Officers' Club No. 2. The verdict "broke the camel's back" of segregation in the military.

In Terry's words:

> *We think it broke the camel's back because they had to recognize the fact that one hundred four officers were arrested, and that they all defied this order, and the order was said to be illegal. We feel, and I think I speak for most of the guys, that it was our advantage that we gave to the Negro people, that there would be no discrimination in the Army Air Force from that time on.*

FOUR

The Code Talkers

Communication is essential in war. When fighting battles, commanders need to be able to communicate with soldiers, and soldiers need to be able to communicate with each other. At the same time, the enemy is listening in, trying to intercept messages and learn about plans even before they begin. The Japanese proved to be especially good at deciphering the Allies's codes. No matter how complicated the message, the Japanese seemed like they were always able to read it and know what the Allies were going to do.

The Allies made their codes more and more difficult. The Japanese had a harder time deciphering them, but the Allies also had a harder time sending them. Sometimes it would take hours to send a message, but in battle, every second counts. The Allies needed a code that the Japanese would not be able to break, but would still be simple enough to send quickly.

***Opposite*: A Navajo family at home on the Navajo reservation during World War II**

THE IDEA

Philip Johnston was working as an engineer in Los Angeles during World War II. He read about the need to create a new code and got the idea to base a code on the Navajo language. Johnston was a veteran of World War I, so he knew the importance of codes and communication. He also knew that Native American languages had been used to build codes before. Most importantly, he knew how to speak Navajo. He was the son of missionaries, and he had grown up around Navajo people. At the time, he was only one of thirty non-Navajos in the world who were able to speak and understand Navajo. He knew that it was impossible to understand if you had not grown up around it. He thought it would make for an excellent code.

"DO YOU HEAR NAVAJO?"

Navajo is a complex language, and even when it is not coded, it is one of the most difficult languages in the world to learn. To speak Navajo, one must be around it for years. It does not have an alphabet, so people learn it by speaking it and listening to it. Navajo speakers don't ask whether or not someone can speak their language, they ask whether or not someone can *hear* their language. Many Navajo sounds are almost impossible to understand unless they are heard again and again and again.

In Navajo, each syllable has a particular tone: high, low, rising, or falling. If that tone is not pronounced correctly, the meaning of the word changes. This nuance, and the fact that so few people knew how to speak it, meant that Navajo did, indeed, make the perfect language with which to write an unbreakable code.

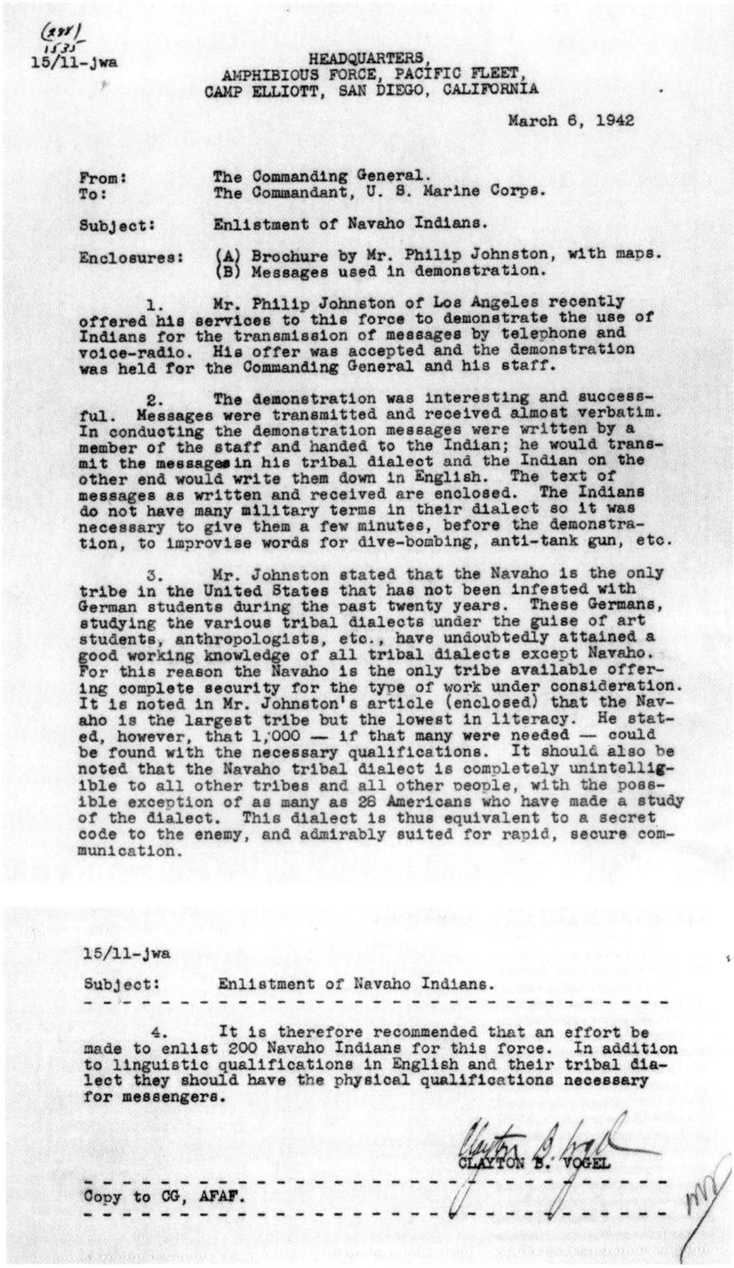

15/11-jwa

HEADQUARTERS,
AMPHIBIOUS FORCE, PACIFIC FLEET,
CAMP ELLIOTT, SAN DIEGO, CALIFORNIA

March 6, 1942

From: The Commanding General.
To: The Commandant, U. S. Marine Corps.

Subject: Enlistment of Navaho Indians.

Enclosures: (A) Brochure by Mr. Philip Johnston, with maps.
(B) Messages used in demonstration.

1. Mr. Philip Johnston of Los Angeles recently offered his services to this force to demonstrate the use of Indians for the transmission of messages by telephone and voice-radio. His offer was accepted and the demonstration was held for the Commanding General and his staff.

2. The demonstration was interesting and successful. Messages were transmitted and received almost verbatim. In conducting the demonstration messages were written by a member of the staff and handed to the Indian; he would transmit the messages in his tribal dialect and the Indian on the other end would write them down in English. The text of messages as written and received are enclosed. The Indians do not have many military terms in their dialect so it was necessary to give them a few minutes, before the demonstration, to improvise words for dive-bombing, anti-tank gun, etc.

3. Mr. Johnston stated that the Navaho is the only tribe in the United States that has not been infested with German students during the past twenty years. These Germans, studying the various tribal dialects under the guise of art students, anthropologists, etc., have undoubtedly attained a good working knowledge of all tribal dialects except Navaho. For this reason the Navaho is the only tribe available offering complete security for the type of work under consideration. It is noted in Mr. Johnston's article (enclosed) that the Navaho is the largest tribe but the lowest in literacy. He stated, however, that 1,000 — if that many were needed — could be found with the necessary qualifications. It should also be noted that the Navaho tribal dialect is completely unintelligible to all other tribes and all other people, with the possible exception of as many as 28 Americans who have made a study of the dialect. This dialect is thus equivalent to a secret code to the enemy, and admirably suited for rapid, secure communication.

15/11-jwa

Subject: Enlistment of Navaho Indians.

4. It is therefore recommended that an effort be made to enlist 200 Navaho Indians for this force. In addition to linguistic qualifications in English and their tribal dialect they should have the physical qualifications necessary for messengers.

CLAYTON B. VOGEL

Copy to CG, AFAF.

Records of Philip Johnston's efforts to use the Navajo language as code

The sounds of Navajo are exact, and the meanings of the words are also exact. For example, if one wanted to say, "I picked something up," the verb "pick up" would be different depending on the object that was picked up. Navajo is more precise and more descriptive than English. The experience of picking up a rock is different than the experience of picking up dirt, so a different verb is used. There are also different verb forms depending on if one, two, three, or more people are picking up the object in question.

CRAFTING THE CODE

Philip Johnston met with Lieutenant James E. Jones of the marines and shared his idea of creating and unbreakable code. Jones listened, but was skeptical. "In all the history of warfare, that has never been done," he said, "No code, no cipher is completely secure from enemy interception." Johnston pressed his case, and eventually persuaded Jones to set up a test.

Johnston found a group of four Navajo to volunteer for the demonstration. The test, conducted at Camp Elliot near San Diego, simulated battlefield conditions, and the volunteers proved that they could encode, send, and decode a three-line message in fewer than thirty seconds. In comparison, the fastest encoding machines at the time took thirty minutes to send and read the same message. The marines didn't need any more convincing. They went looking for recruits.

THE CODE TALKERS

Major General Clayton Vogel, the commanding officer at Camp Elliot, sent a letter to the marine commandant in Washington, DC, describing the need for a better code, and, based on the successful demonstration, requested two hundred recruits be trained as code talkers. He was given permission to recruit up to thirty.

Several white marines who'd grown up on or around the Navajo Reservation and could understand and speak some Navajo volunteered to be code talkers. However, no matter how fluent they were, there were some tones and sounds that they couldn't quite pronounce or understand. Given that there was no margin for error when it came to communicating in combat, the non-Navajos were not chosen as code talkers.

Twenty-nine Navajo recruits made up the first group of code talkers. They did not know that they had been recruited to create a secret code; they only knew that they were going to join the marines. For many of the recruits, going to basic training was the first time they had been off the reservation, their first time out of state, or even their first time on a bus. Their first stop was Camp Pendleton in Southern California. They were officially the 382nd Platoon of the United States Marine Corps.

Basic training is difficult for any recruit, and the Navajo struggled to make the adjustment. The physical challenges were not the problem; most Navajo were used to hard work. It was more difficult for the Navajo to make the necessary cultural changes. For example, Navajo men traditionally wore their hair long, but in the marines they had to cut it short. In addition, Navajos felt that making eye contact with someone was disrespectful, but in the marines it was a sign of good discipline. In spite of these obstacles, all twenty-nine recruits made it through basic training.

THE LONG WALK

That the United States Military needed the help of the Navajo—and in particular their language—was an interesting twist of history to say the least. In 1848, the United States Army invaded Navajo territory and, though the Navajo resisted for years, eventually forced the Navajo off their land. Thousands of Navajo were forced to walk hundreds of miles. Many died along the way. Navajos refer to this forced march as the Long Walk.

Four years after the Long Walk, the Navajo returned to their land, but they were forced to stay on a reservation and adopt a new, more American way of life. Navajo children were sent to boarding schools where they were made to dress and act like Americans. They were forced to change the way they dressed, they were given different names, they were made to change their hair, and they were forbidden from speaking Navajo.

When Samuel Tso, an original code talker, who grew up going to boarding school, learned he was supposed to make a code using his native language, he remembers thinking, "Hey you didn't want me to speak my language. How come? Now you want it?"

Luckily for the United States, its attempt to eradicate Navajo culture and language failed. Navajo people held on to their traditional values and their native language. Many Navajo enlisted in the military because their values taught them that warriors must protect their people. The Navajo language was so

Many code talkers grew up going to government-run boarding schools.

rich and complicated that it made for a perfect code. Therefore, Navajo culture and Navajo language were essential to winning World War II.

Chester Nez, also an original code talker, described what made Navajo culture and language so uniquely suited to code talking:

> *Despite the efforts of boarding schools to repress it, Navajo oral tradition remained strong. Stories were told around the campfires at home, memorized, and told again ... and again. Memorization, for each of us, was second nature.*
>
> *And, again, despite the efforts of boarding schools, from the time of their birth, Navajo children in a traditional environment were exposed to the exacting and complex thought process required by the Navajo language. This helped contribute to their ability to deal with decisions and complexities in their lives. Certainly it contributed to the abilities required to be a code talker: learning quickly, memorizing, and working under extreme pressure. I am thankful that my father and grandparents taught me my Navajo language well.*

THE CODE

After they completed basic training, the twenty-nine Navajo recruits were sent to Camp Elliot. It was there that they learned that they had been recruited to build a new code using their native language.

As Chester Nez said, "The brass came by and told us to use our language to come up with words representing the letters A to Z, and to come up with a code for military terms.

By deciphering coded messages, the Japanese military could learn of Allied plans ahead of time. The US needed an unbreakable code.

They put us in a room to work it out and, at first, everybody thought we'd never make it. It seemed impossible because even among ourselves, we didn't agree on the right Navajo words."

One of the first problems they encountered was the fact that many English words did not have a Navajo equivalent.

Therefore, the code talkers had to give Navajo names to things like submarines (*besh-lo*, "iron fish") and fighter planes (*dah-he-tih-hi*, "hummingbird"), and decide on a way to write those words using English letters. Then, they had to figure out how to use Navajo words to represent English letters.

For example, a tank could be called a *chay-da-gahi* (tortoise), or it could be spelled out using the code *than-zi* (Turkey), *tse-nill* (Ax), *tsah* (Needle), *klizzie-yazzie* (Kid). To make the code even more elaborate, the code talkers used three different words for each English letter. The letter A was "ant," "apple," or "ax,"—in Navajo, *wol-la-chee*, *be-la-sana*, or *tse-nill*. Since different Navajo words could be used for the same English letter, "tank" would never be coded the same way twice. Though the code talkers might be saying "tank" over and over again, it would always sound different to anyone listening in on the message.

Along with creating the code, the code talkers had to learn how use and repair the radios they used to send the messages. Wireless technology was still relatively new. The code talkers blended their old language with the latest technology to create an indispensable way to communicate in battle. They practiced using the radio to send the code until they were able to send and translate three lines of code with making any mistakes.

The original recruits were so successful, and the marines were so impressed with their skills, that marine corps leaders put in an order for more code talkers to be recruited. Philip Johnston was in charge of recruiting, and two of the original twenty-nine, Johnny Manuelito and John Benally, were asked to stay at Camp Elliot and teach the new recruits. Before long, there were more than four hundred code talkers.

GOING TO BATTLE

The code talkers first went to battle in the summer of 1942. They served in all six marine divisions in the Pacific, and were part of every marine assault from 1942 until the end of the war in 1945. They were usually on the front lines among the first soldiers to go into battle, because they had to get into position and set up their radios so they could communicate with other troops. The code talkers sent messages about locations, reported on the progress of the battle, and sent for reinforcements when they were needed. The Japanese military was quite skilled at locating radio signals, so the code talkers had to move quickly: finding a position, setting up the equipment, sending, receiving, and translating messages, and then packing up the equipment and running to a new location before they were discovered.

The code talkers played a part in every battle in the Pacific, but it was during the battle for Iwo Jima that they really proved how important they were. Six code talkers fought with the marines during the Battle of Iwo Jima. The code talkers were not only helpful during the battle, they were vital. Major Howard Conner, the Fifth Marine Division's Signal Officer, said that "The entire operation was directed by Navajo code ... During the two days that followed the initial landings I had six Navajo radio nets working around the clock ... They sent and received over 800 messages without an error. Were it not for the Navajo Code Talkers, the Marines never would have taken Iwo Jima."

As Chester Nez put it, "The Navajo code words were never written when we transmitted messages. That made us men living, walking code machines ... if the Navajo oral tradition had not been as strong as it was, human error could have

Code talkers had to be technically skilled and physically fit.

rendered this method of communication impractical … As far as I know, we generally transmitted our messages flawlessly. If someone did make an error, someone else in the Navajo network would catch it and send an alert. And we never relaxed, never let up."

Samuel Tso was at Iwo Jima, and he describes the role of the code talkers:

> *The radiomen, they always said, "Message for Arizona!" And that meant a code talker needed to receive it … Message for Arizona. Can you hear it? You can't read it. You can't write it. You have to decode it in your head and change it to English.*
>
> *Our mission was to locate [a] machine gun. [Two other] code talkers sent the coordinates and ordered mortar fire, rocket fire, and artillery fire, all three at the same time, at one machine gun nest. Within five minutes you could hear all the explosions coming in, you could see rockets coming over … Rocks were flying all over the place.*

As skilled as they were at breaking code, the Japanese were never able to break the Navajo code. According to a Japanese newspaper, the code sounded like "a strange earful of gurgling noises … resembling the call of a Tibetan monk and the sound of a hot water bottle being emptied." At one point, the Japanese captured a Navajo soldier who was not a code talker. They held him prisoner and forced him to listen to the code and tell them what it said. Even though he could

“As a Warrior …”

Even though he could have stayed home and finished high school, Marine-Private First Class Chester Nez enlisted in the marines as a code talker. He had never seen the ocean, much less been on a ship, before being deployed to the Pacific. He recalls in his memoir *Code Talker: The First and Only Memoir by One of the Original Navajo Code Talkers of WWII*, how he drew on his Navajo upbringing to give him strength as he sailed toward the Battle of Guadalcanal:

> *I'd always believed in the "Right Way." Balance must be found … I reminded myself that my Navajo people had always been warriors, protectors. In that, there was honor. I would concentrate on being a warrior and on protecting my homeland.*

Even though his clothes were always damp, and his stomach was always queasy, Nez knew that he had made a good choice, the right choice. He knew that part of being a Navajo was being a warrior, and being a warrior meant protecting his people: “I could have stayed in high school, I thought. Maybe I should have. But, as a warrior, how could I ignore the fact that my country had been attacked?”

understand the words, he did not know the code, so he was unable to understand the messages.

After the war ended, the *Fuji Evening*, a newspaper in Tokyo wrote that, "If the Japanese Imperial Intelligence Team could have decoded the Navajo messages … the history of the Pacific War might have turned out completely different."

FIVE

A Hero's Welcome?

What happens to a dream deferred?
Does it dry up
like a raisin in the sun?
—Langston Hughes, "Harlem" (1951)

A DREAM DEFERRED

When they returned from World War II, the Tuskegee Airmen and other black service men found that although they had been fighting for freedom overseas, freedom was not waiting for them when they got home. Back in the United States, they found Jim Crow segregation and economic inequality. The lofty ideals for which they fought, and for which many died, were still just ideas, and they were not being practiced.

Alex Jefferson, one of the Airmen, was held as a prisoner of war in Germany. Though the Germans did not treat him well, they treated him with more respect than the average white

***Opposite*: One of the original code talkers receives the Congressional Medal of Honor in 2001.**

soldier in his own army. After the Allies won the war, and he was freed, he returned home. He felt joy and pride when his ship pulled into New York Harbor. When he got off the ship, however, he was told, "Whites to the right, Negroes to the left." "Back to the United States," he said to himself.

In the military itself, equality was hard to come by, particularly among officers. In the army, there was only one black officer for every seventy black enlisted men. For white personnel, the ratio was one officer for every seven enlisted men. In the other branches of the military, there was even more of a disparity.

Soon after the war, the military was reorganized, and the air force became a separate branch. Prior to that it had been part of the army. The air force had the chance to prove that it was more forward-thinking than the army, able to innovate and recognize the wisdom of new ideas. There was also pressure from civil rights groups, demanding that the United States live up to its own standards, especially given that it saw itself as the new global leader and a beacon of freedom and democracy.

There was a great deal of resistance to integrating the air force, or any other branch of the military. In spite of the Tuskegee Airmen's proven success, people like Colonel Selway refused to acknowledge that blacks were equal to whites. He wrote that black soldiers lack initiative, and could not succeed without the supervision of a white officer.

Other leaders, however, recognized the fact that black pilots had all the skills necessary to succeed, and black people's demands for equality were not going to go away. The war hero Colonel James Doolittle advised the military that, "You are merely postponing the inevitable, and you might as well take it gracefully." Noel Parrish, a white officer who had long favored equality, reminded opponents of integration, "Whether we like or dislike Negroes and whether they like or dislike us, under the Constitution of the United States, which we are all sworn to uphold, they are citizens of the United States having the same rights and privileges of other citizens and entitled to the same applications and protection of the laws."

With pressure building within the military, with civil rights leaders like A. Philip Randolph threatening to march thousands of people through Washington, and with Congress unwilling

Rosa Parks led the Montgomery Bus Boycott, one of the earliest and most successful Civil Rights campaigns.

to pass legislation, President Truman signed an executive order directing the Secretary of Defense to desegregate the military as quickly as possible. "It is hereby declared to be the policy of the President that there shall be equality of treatment and opportunity for all persons in the armed services without regard to race, color, or religion or national origin. This policy shall be put into effect as rapidly as possible, having due regard to the time required to effectuate any necessary changes without impairing efficiency or morale."

In the decades after World War II, the Civil Rights movement fought for integration, economic justice, and voting rights.

Not long after the air force was integrated, the Tuskegee Air Field shut down because there was no longer any need for a separate training facility for blacks only. This was, at the same time, a loss of a black institution and a sign of progress. There were no longer black military academies and white military academies, there were only military academies where all were welcome and trained and graduated according to their ability. Down the road from Tuskegee was Montgomery, Alabama. In that town, the battle for integration was just beginning. The Montgomery Improvement Association formed with a mission to advance human rights for African Americans in that city. One of their first actions was the famous bus **boycott,** led by Rosa Parks. The Tuskegee Airmen were not part of this boycott, but they paved the way for the boycott and for all of the progress that came after them.

In the decades that followed World War II, African Americans and their allies continued to fight for integration, and beyond that, justice in other areas, such as voting rights. They fought against their fellow Americans who did not want black Americans to be integrated and did not want to make it easy for black Americans to vote.

The Civil Rights movement was nonviolent, but that does not mean it was nonconfrontational. Many Civil Rights leaders, like Martin Luther King Jr. and Malcom X, questioned why black soldiers should be sent to other countries to fight for freedoms they didn't enjoy at home. Sometimes protesters would be attacked by the police or counter-protestors. Many Civil Rights leaders were killed for speaking out. The movement won some important victories, such as the Voting Rights Act in 1965, but even today movements for racial and economic justice continue in all parts of the country.

JUSTICE IN THE FIELDS

African Americans were not the only group fighting for equal rights after World War II. Following the war and the ensuing economic expansion, many more Mexicans moved to the United States to find work and support their families. Though many crossed over illegally, Mexican workers were an important part of the local economy. Often when they were arrested, white farmers and ranchers would complain to the Border Patrol. The ranchers and farmers liked having the cheap labor, and they would often bargain to get the workers released.

In the mid-1950s, the economy slowed, and then shrank. During the recession, there were fewer jobs, and more pressure to deport people who crossed the border illegally. President Eisenhower and his administration launched "Operation Wetback" (Wetback is a derogatory term for a Mexican laborer). Border Patrol agents and local police in California, Arizona, New Mexico, and Texas deported over one million people, some of whom were here illegally, but many of whom were American citizens who were supposed to have Constitutional rights.

It was not the first time Mexicans and Mexican Americans faced mass-deportation, but this time they pushed back. Mexicans and Mexican Americans fought in World War II, and they had worked in farms and factories to support the war effort. They were an important part of the United States, and they wanted their rights.

The American GI Forum (AGIF) was formed in 1948 to address the needs of Mexican American veterans, because

Dolores Huerta (*left*) and Cesar Chavez (*right*), leaders of the United Farm Workers

Department of Veterans Affairs was denying their requests for medical treatment. The AGIF moved beyond veterans' issues and also addressed issues like fair housing, voting rights, and school segregation. It was an early piece of a larger movement for Mexican American rights.

Activists won several major victories in the decade after World War II, including the 1947 *Mendez vs. Westminster* Supreme Court ruling, which declared that segregating Latino children was unconstitutional, and the 1954 *Hernandez vs. Texas* ruling, which declared that Latinos were entitled to equal protection under the Constitution.

The movement for Mexican American rights was called the Chicano Movement. The movement, which traced its roots back to the mid-nineteenth century, really took shape in the 1940s. The term *chicano* was originally a derogatory term used to describe the children of Mexican immigrants. Children born to immigrants felt out of place on either side of the border. They were not "really Americans" nor were they "really Mexicans." To claim their unique identity, they embraced the word that was once used to single them out. They were chicanos, and proud of it.

The movement reached its peak in the mid-1960s through the mid-1970s. Activists organized **strikes**, marches, rallies, and sit-ins in many parts of the country. The most powerful organization to come out of the movement was the United Farm Workers (UFW), led by Cesar Chavez and Dolores Huerta.

Dolores Huerta was not always an organizer. She began her career as a teacher in Stockton, California. Every day, she watched as her students came to school in ragged clothing. Often her students were underfed and in poor health. She knew it wasn't her students' fault, and it wasn't their parents' fault, either. The parents were working as hard as they could to make a living and provide for their families. In order to improve the lives of her students, Huerta needed to improve the lives of their families. She needed to improve the wages and working conditions of the fields in which they worked.

"The work was hard and dangerous," she said. "Crop dusters sprayed pesticides on the fields while people were working. People got really sick, and some died … I couldn't stand seeing kids come to class hungry and needing shoes. I thought I could do more by organizing farm workers than by trying to teach their hungry children."

Cesar Chavez was a third-generation Mexican American. His grandparents moved to Arizona in the 1880s. His father owned and operated many small businesses, among them a freight business, a grocery store, and a pool hall. Then came the Great Depression, which wiped out all the businesses,

Migrant farm workers labor in harsh conditions for very little pay.

Women in the Military

Women from all backgrounds also served in the military during World War II. Though they did not see combat, 350,000 women joined the Armed Forces. The members of the Women's Army Corps (WAC) served in the United States and in Europe, Asia, and North Africa. In the navy, women signed up for Women Accepted for Volunteer Emergency Service (WAVES). The coast guard and marine corps also had similar programs.

Women also served as Women's Air Force Service Pilots (WASPs). They flew military planes from factories to bases, as well as transported goods to combat zones. In addition, they flew in combat simulation and training exercises. Over 1,000 WASPs flew in World War II; they were the first American military pilots.

Beyond the military, women were active on the home front, joining the workforce like never before. For example, before the war 1 percent of the aviation manufacturing industry was female. During the war, that number jumped to 60 percent. The munitions industry also recruited large numbers of women to build weapons. The government's recruitment campaign used a character called Rosie the Riveter, a muscle-flexing, bandana-wearing woman. Rosie became a symbol of female strength.

Women, like other minority groups, came out of the war with a new sense of their own power. Having stepped forward, they were not ready to step back. After the war, Rosie the

Rosie the Riveter

Riveter became an iconic symbol of the Women's Movement, which fought for, among other things, equal pay for women, who proved that they could do the same work as men.

along with much of the American economy. His family moved around after that, taking whatever work they could find, much of it in the fields.

When he began organizing farm workers, he did so as an insider. He had lived their life. He was one of them. "It was [a hard] life. Working in the fields in the scorching hot summers. Living in a broken-down car, or else in the dark, overcrowded shacks without toilets, electricity, or running water."

The workers in the fields grew the food that fed the nation, yet those workers were paid next to nothing and had few, if any, protections. Chavez formed the National Farm Workers Union with the goal of giving workers the dignity that they had earned. "I have been driven by one dream, one goal, one vision: to overthrow a farm labor system … which treats farm workers as if they were not important human beings."

The UFW was a merger of the National Farm Workers Union and the Filipino Agricultural Workers Organizing Committee. Using the same strategy of nonviolent resistance that Martin Luther King Jr. and other civil rights leaders used, the UFW fought to improve the poor wages and working conditions of all farm workers.

In 1965, the UFW confronted grape growers in Delano, California. Demanding they be paid minimum wage, Filipino workers walked off the job, leaving the grapes to rot on the vine. The growers did not want to negotiate, however, so they bused in more workers to harvest the grapes. The farm workers themselves did not have enough leverage to force the growers to bargain with them. They needed a broader movement that had the support of people from many walks of life.

The UFW organized a strike in California, and a boycott throughout the rest of the country. In the fields the striking workers were attacked by strikebreakers who drove pickup trucks into picket lines and sprayed workers with pesticides. All the while, the workers remained nonviolent, kneeling and praying in the face of the attacks. In the rest of the country, the UFW coordinated with students, churches, and other unions and civic groups to win support for a boycott: grapes first, and then lettuce. At the same time, Chavez went on a series of hunger strikes to draw attention to the cause.

The UFW won widespread support for their cause. The pressure from the strike, the boycott, and the publicity generated by the hunger strikes, forced the growers to negotiate with the farm workers. The new contracts meant better wages and working conditions for all the farm workers in the California fields.

"OUR PLACE IN THE SUN"

In December 1944, the US Supreme Court issued a new ruling on the legality of the Japanese Internment Camps, stating that the War Relocation Authority did not have the power "to detain citizens against whom no charges of disloyalty … have been made for a period longer than that necessary to separate the loyal from the disloyal." Soon after that, on January 2, 1945, Major General Henry Pratt made Public Proclamation No. 21, which said that Japanese Americans who had been forced into internment camps could return home.

Many families had no home to return to, however. They had lost their homes and most of their property when they were forced to relocate. Even detainees that were able to return home had to face the lingering fear and prejudice that many Americans held for Japanese and Japanese American people. Yori Kochiyama recalls:

> *I returned [home] in October of 1945. It was very hard to find work, at least for me. I wasn't expecting to find anything good, just something to tide me over until my boyfriend came back from New York. The only thing I was looking for was to work in a restaurant as a waitress. But I couldn't find anything. I would walk from one end of the town to the other, and down every main avenue. But as soon as they found out I was Japanese, they would say no ... So finally what I did was go to the rough area of San Pedro ... I was determined to keep the jobs as long as I could ... I could last maybe two hours, and somebody would say "Is that a Jap?" And as soon as someone would ask that, the boss would say, "Sorry, you gotta go. We don't want no trouble here."*

In 1948, Congress passed the Japanese Claims Act. In June, President Truman signed it into law. The law authorized the settlement of claims made by people who lost wealth and property when they were relocated. In passing the law, Congress and the President acknowledged the interment was wrong and harmful, and Japanese Americans deserved compensation.

During the war, the 442nd Regimental Combat Team, made up of Japanese and Japanese American soldiers, many with family members in the camps, fought for the United States. They saw combat in Italy, France, and Germany. Not only did the 442nd fight, they fought well. Over fourteen thousand men served in the 442nd. By the end of the war, it was one of the most decorated units of its size in US military history. The 442nd earned 9,486 Purple Hearts, eight Presidential Unit Citations, and twenty-one Medals of Honor.

Japanese Americans also made up most the 100th Infantry Battalion. Most members of the 100th were former Members of the Hawaii Army National Guard. When veterans of the 100th and 442nd returned to the United States, they were not willing to go back to being second class citizens. They had fought for their country, proved their bravery and loyalty, and they were ready to take their place as equal members of society.

In Hawaii, especially, veterans came back eager for change. Hawaii, at the time, was a territory of the United States, and the economy and government were dominated by the "Big Five" sugarcane processing corporations. These corporations conspired to keep prices high and wages low. The Big Five also had strong ties to the Republican Party of Hawaii, so the returning veterans and other organizations working for change aligned with the Democratic Party.

In 1954, a series of protests, strikes, and other acts of civil disobedience broke the power of the Big Five. The Hawaii Democratic Revolution of 1954 paved the way for elections that ended with the Republican Party being voted out of office and the Democratic Party taking control. As part of their push for full equality, activists and organizers pushed for full statehood. There was some opposition and concern in the rest of the country, particularly among the southern states, due to the Communist Party of Hawaii's participation in the 1954 protests. However, in 1959, Congress passed the Hawaii Admission Act, and President Eisenhower signed it into law.

When the people of Hawaii voted on the issue, they voted 94.3 percent in favor of statehood.

Daniel Inouye was one of the veterans of the 442nd who returned to Hawaii and took part in the 1954 uprising. "We knew we were expendable," explained Inouye, "but we knew that we had to pay that price … and we were willing to pay that price … but once we paid that price we wanted our place in the sun." After Hawaii was granted statehood, Inouye became the first Japanese American to be elected to the House of Representatives. Three years later he was elected Senator. He served in the Senate until his death in 2012.

DECLASSIFIED CODE TALK

Thirteen of the more than four hundred code talkers were killed in action. At the end of the war, the rest of the code talkers quietly returned home and went about their lives. The marines wanted to be able to use the code in future wars, if necessary, so the code talker project remained classified. The code talkers were not allowed to talk about the code with anyone, not even friends and family. The code talkers did not receive any awards or recognition of any kind.

When Chester Nez returned home, his friends asked him what he did during the war. "The Marines issued me a gun and some ammunition and told me to go hunt down and kill some Japanese," was all he could say. He couldn't mention the code he helped write.

When the Korean War broke out in 1950, Nez and other code talkers were called back into service. Unlike World War II, the Korean War ended relatively quickly and the secret code never needed to be used. The code talkers were never sent into battle.

By 1968, modern equipment and new encryption techniques meant that the marines would no longer need to use the Navajo code, and would therefore no longer need to keep it a secret. The code talker project was finally declassified, and the rest of the country finally learned about important contribution that Navajo people made to the war. In 1982, President Reagan declared that August 14 was National Navajo Code Talker Day. In April of 2000, Senator Jeff Bingaman of New Mexico proposed an act to honor the code talkers for their heroic action and the unique service they provided. On December 22, 2000, President Clinton signed the bill into law. On July 26, 2001, President Bush gave Congressional medals to each of the original twenty-nine code talkers. Only five of the twenty-nine were still alive to receive the honor in person. Later that same year, Congressional medals were given to each of the rest of the code talkers.

"But there's one thing that's especially good," Nez said, "My fellow code talkers and I have become a part of a new oral and written tradition, a Navajo victory, with our culture contributing to our country's defeat of a wily foe. The story of the code talkers has been told on the Checkerboard and the reservation and recorded in the pages of history books forever. Our story is not one of sorrow, like the Long Walk and the Great Livestock Massacre, but one of triumph."

Glossary

Allies The United States, Great Britain, The Soviet Union, and other countries that fought against the Axis Powers (Japan, Italy, Germany) during World War II.

authoritarian Favoring or enforcing strict obedience to authority.

autonomous Country or region having self-governance.

Axis Japan, Germany, Italy. They fought against the United States and other Allies during World War II.

barrack A building where military personnel live.

boycott To refuse to buy something as way of protest.

braceros Mexican workers allowed into the United States for a certain amount of time.

Communists Proponents of a centralized political and economic system in which all wealth is publicly owned.

enlist To sign up for the armed services.

fascists Proponents of an authoritarian and nationalist form of government.

front The farthest position that an army has reached; the place they are most likely to encounter an enemy.

ghettos Parts of a city occupied by a minority group.

internment camps Prison camps for people considered enemies during war time.

Luftwaffe The German Air Force during World War II.

offensive An attacking military campaign.

pachuco A 1940s slang term for a young Mexican American man.

pact A formal agreement between two people or groups.

peninsula A piece of land almost completely surrounded by water.

rationed When a fixed amount of food or other commodity is allowed to a person during a shortage.

reinforcements Extra soldiers sent to increase the strength of an army.

republic A political system in which power is held by the people and their elected representatives.

reservations Clearly defined zones in which Native Americans were forced to live.

segregation The action of keeping one group of people separate from another.

siege A military blockade of city with the intent of forcing the citizens of the city to surrender.

squadron A unit in the air force containing a certain number of aircraft and their crews.

stalemate A situation is which neither side is winning a conflict.

strike A refusal to work by an organized group of workers.

treaty A formal peace agreement between two nations.

veteran A person who has served in the military.

zoot suit A style of suit popular in the 1930s and 1940s known for its baggy pants and wide shoulders.

Bibliography

Fountain, Nigel. *WWII: The People's Story*. Pleasantville, New York: Reader's Digest, 2003.

Francis, Charles E. *Tuskegee Airmen: The Men Who Changed a Nation*. Boston: Branden Books, 2008.

Lord, James. *My Queer War*. New York: Farrar, Strauss, and Giroux, 2010.

Moye, J. Todd. *Freedom Flyers: The Tuskegee Airmen of World War II*. New York: Oxford University Press, 2010.

Nez, Chester, and Judith Schiess Avila. *Code Talker: The First and Only Memoir by One of the Original Navajo Code Talkers of WWII*. New York: Berkley Books, 2011.

Santella, Andrew. *Navajo Code Talkers*. Minneapolis, Minnesota: Compass Point Books, 2004.

Sloan, Bill. *The Ultimate Battle: Okinawa 1945-The Last Epic Struggle of World War II*. New York: Simon & Schuster Paperbacks, 2007.

Smith, Larry. *Iwo Jima: World War II Veterans Remember the Greatest Battle of the Pacific*. New York: W.W. Norton & Company, 2008.

Stavans, Ilan. *Latino History and Culture*. New York: HarperCollins, 2007.

Suarez, Ray. *Latino Americans: The 500-Year Legacy That Shaped a Nation.* New York: Celebra, 2013.

Sullivan, Patricia. *Lift Every Voice: The NAACP and the Making of the Civil Rights Movement.* New York: The New Press, 2009.

Valk, Anne, and Leslie Brown. *Living with Jim Crow: African American Women and Memories of the Segregated South.* New York: Palgrave MacMillan, 2010.

Willis, Clarence E. *African American Voices from Iwo Jima: Personal Accounts of the Battle.* Jefferson, North Carolina: McFarland & Company, Inc., 2010.

Zinn, Howard. *A People's History of the United States.* New York: HarperPerennial, 2003.

Zinn, Howard, and Anthony Arnove. *Voices of a People's History of the United States.* New York: Seven Stories Press, 2009.

Further Information

Websites

Go for Broke: National Education Center

http://www.goforbroke.org/

Learn about the history of Japanese American regiments from World War II with interactive maps and descriptions of the campaigns they were involved in. Also find an oral history video archive

History: World War II

http://www.bbc.co.uk/history/worldwars/wwtwo
Find information on the Second World War in the form of audio recordings, photo galleries, and animated maps and timelines.

Race and the Army During World War II

http://www.pbs.org/wgbh/amex/alaska/peopleevents/e_army.html

PBS provides a survey of the African American struggle to break through racial barriers in World War II. This site includes a link to Truman's executive order to desegregate the military.

The Voces Oral History Project

http://www.lib.utexas.edu/voces/

This project was organized by the University of Texas at Austin to capture the stories of Latinos and Latinas during World War II. The website features web versions of the academic journal that was published from 1999 to 2004. Issues contain the narratives of soldiers and civilians involved in the war effort.

Videos

Shindler's List (Amblin Entertainment, 1993)
This movie is based on the true story of Oskar Shindler, a German businessman who risked his life to hide thousands of Jewish people during World War Two.

The War (Florentine Films, 2007) This mini-series that tells the stories of the soldiers who fought in the war and the people who stayed behind.

Books

Hillenbrand, Laura. *Unbroken: A World War II Story of Survival, Resilience, and Redemption.* New York: Random House, 2010.

Houston, Jeanne Wakatsuki. *Farewell to Manzanar: A True Story of Japanese American Experience During and After World War II Internment.* New York: Houghton Mifflin, 1973.

Krull, Kathleen and Yuyi Morales. *Harvesting Hope: The Story of Cesar Chavez.* New York: HarcourtBooks, 2003.

Lewis, J. Patrick and Gary Kelley. *The Navajo Code Talkers.* Mankato, Minnesota: Creative Editions, 2016.

Index

Page numbers in **boldface** are illustrations. Entries in **boldface** are glossary terms.

About the Author

Matt Lang was raised in western Pennsylvania. He went to college in Erie, Pennsylvania, transferred to the College of Wooster, and in time, moved to Chicago, where he now lives in an intentional community with many other people, including his wife and daughter.

Lang is the author of *The Giraffe's Mustache: A Storybook You Can Color, McKean County and Other Stories,* and *Fernweh.*